W9-DGN-083

States

TEXAS

by Bridget Parker

CAPSTONE PRESS
a capstone imprint

Next Page Books are published by Capstone Press,
1710 Roe Crest Drive, North Mankato, Minnesota 56003
www.mycapstone.com

Copyright © 2017 by Capstone Press, a Capstone imprint. All rights
reserved. No part of this publication may be reproduced in whole or
in part, or stored in a retrieval system, or transmitted in any form
or by any means, electronic, mechanical, photocopying, recording, or
otherwise, without written permission of the publisher.

Library of Congress Cataloging-in-Publication Data
Cataloging-in-publication information is on file with the Library of
Congress.
ISBN 978-1-5157-0431-7 (library binding)
ISBN 978-1-5157-0490-4 (paperback)
ISBN 978-1-5157-0542-0 (ebook PDF)

Editorial Credits
Jaclyn Jaycox, editor; Kazuko Collins and Katy LaVigne, designers;
Morgan Walters, media researcher; Tori Abraham, production specialist

Photo Credits
Capstone Press: Angi Gahler, map 4, 7; CriaImages.com: Jay Robert
Nash Collection, middle 18, bottom 18; Dreamstime: Jerry Coli,
middle 19, Paul Sankey, 28; Newscom: LARRY W. SMITH/EPA, 10,
Richard Cummins/robertharding, 11, ZOJ WENN Photos/JLC, top 18;
North Wind Picture Archives, 26; One Mile Up, Inc., flag, seal 23;
Shutterstock: Arto Hakola, top left 21, Bruce Raynor, middle left 21,
cholder, top 24, Christopher Halloran, bottom 19, Dean Fikar, bottom
left 8, 9, Dorti, top right 20, Everett Historical, 12, 27, f11photo, 6, 13,
Foodio, bottom right 21, Fred LaBounty, 7, fstockfoto, bottom left 21,
GSPhotography, 16, IrinaK, top left 20, Jill Nightingale, bottom left 20,
Jim Parkin, 15, Jiri Hera, bottom right 20, Joel Shawn, top 19, John
Blanton, 17, Joseph Sohm, bottom 24, Konstantnin, middle right 21,
life_is_fantastic, 29, Marzolino, 25, Randall Stevens, 5, Rusty Dodson,
top right 21, T photography, cover, 14, Wildnerdpix, bottom right 8

All design elements by Shutterstock

Printed in the United States of America
000905

TABLE OF CONTENTS

Want to take your research further? Ask your librarian if your school subscribes to PebbleGo Next. If so, when you see this helpful symbol (↖) throughout the book, log onto www.pebblegonext.com for bonus downloads and information.

LOCATION

Texas is in the southwestern United States. Oklahoma is north of Texas. The Texas Panhandle, the part of Texas that stretches northward, is next to the western part of Oklahoma. Arkansas touches the northeastern corner of Texas. The Red River divides Texas from Oklahoma and Arkansas. Louisiana lies to the east of Texas. New Mexico borders the western side of Texas. The Gulf of Mexico washes against the southeastern side of Texas. The Rio Grande divides the state from Mexico in the south. Texas' capital and fourth-largest city is Austin. The three largest cities are Houston, San Antonio, and Dallas.

PebbleGo Next Bonus!
To print and label
your own map, go to
www.pebblegonext.com
and search keywords:

TX MAP

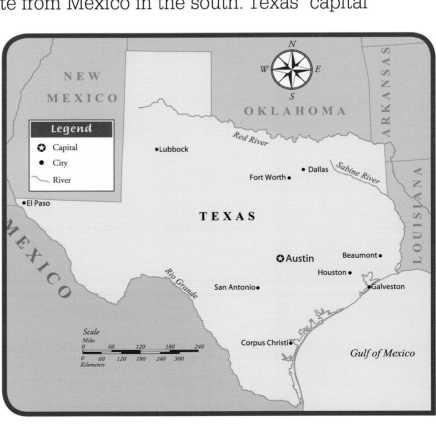

More people visit Austin each year than Disneyland. Nearly 20 million tourists come to the city annually.

GEOGRAPHY

The mountains of western Texas are part of the southern tip of the Rocky Mountains. In this area, the highest point in the state, Guadalupe Peak, reaches 8,749 feet (2,667 meters) above sea level. The Texas Panhandle is the part of Texas that stretches northward. The Great Plains covers the Texas Panhandle and central Texas. The prairies and lakes of central Texas lie east of the Great Plains. The Rio Grande and other rivers flow into the Gulf of Mexico. Long, narrow islands called barrier islands lay along the Gulf Coast.

PebbleGo Next Bonus!
To watch a video about the Alamo, go to www.pebblegonext.com and search keywords:

TX VIDEO

The San Antonio River Walk is a 1.5-mile- (2.4-kilometer-) long waterway lined with paths, cafes, and shops.

Guadalupe Peak is found in the Guadalupe Mountains National Park.

WEATHER

The average summer temperature in Texas is 81 degrees Fahrenheit (27 degrees Celsius). The average winter temperature is 48°F (9°C). Parts of western Texas receive less than 12 inches (30 centimeters) of rain each year. Areas along the Gulf Coast receive up to 50 inches (127 cm) of rain each year.

Average High and Low Temperatures (Austin, TX)

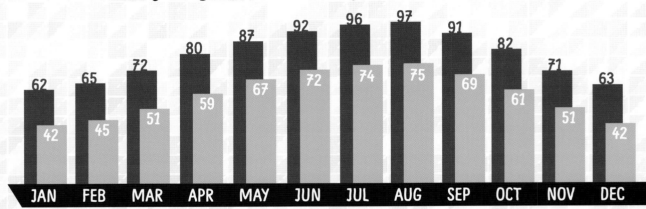

	JAN	FEB	MAR	APR	MAY	JUN	JUL	AUG	SEP	OCT	NOV	DEC
High	62	65	72	80	87	92	96	97	91	82	71	63
Low	42	45	51	59	67	72	74	75	69	61	51	42

LANDMARKS

The Alamo

More than 2.5 million people each year visit the location of the Battle of the Alamo. Located in downtown San Antonio, the Alamo houses exhibits on the Texas Revolution and Texas history.

Six Flags over Texas

Six Flags over Texas in Arlington was the first Six Flags theme park. It has roller coasters and other rides. The park has thousands of visitors each day.

Space Center Houston

At the Visitor Center for NASA's Johnson Space Center, visitors learn about what it's like to live and work in space. They can see where flight controllers communicate with astronauts on the International Space Station and the old mission control facility where NASA monitored the moon landing.

HISTORY AND GOVERNMENT

The roughly 200 defenders of the Alamo were greatly outnumbered. The Mexican army that defeated them had at least 1,800 soldiers.

Spanish explorers were the first Europeans in Texas. In the early 1500s, Hernán Cortés claimed Texas and Mexico for Spain. In 1821 Mexico became its own country and included what is now Texas. Many Americans saw a chance for a better life in Texas. Tension grew between U.S. settlers and the Mexican government. The Texas Revolution began in 1835. A year later the Texans lost the Battle of the Alamo. On March 2 Texans signed their Declaration of Independence. Sam Houston led the Texan army to victory against Mexico in May 1836. Texas remained its own country until December 29, 1845, when it became the 28th U.S. state.

Members of Texas' legislature make laws. The Texas Senate has 31 members and the House of Representatives has 150 members. The governor is the leader of the executive branch. The Texas judicial branch includes the courts, which uphold the laws.

The state capitol building in Austin is pink because of the Sunset Red granite used to build it.

INDUSTRY

Two-thirds of Texas' land covers oil fields. One-third of the petroleum in the United States lies under Texas soil. The state is also the country's top natural gas producer. Besides petroleum and natural gas, Texas also mines coal, Portland cement, and limestone. Texas has more mining jobs than any other state.

Texas has the most cattle of any state. Two-thirds of the state's farmland is used for cattle ranches. The rest of Texas' farmland is used for growing crops. The state's main crop is cotton.

One of the largest cattle ranches in the world is found in Texas. King Ranch covers 825,000 acres (333,866 hectares). That's bigger than Rhode Island!

Manufacturing plants in Texas prepare soft drinks, baked goods, and computers. Texas factories make chemicals for paint, ink, makeup, and fertilizer.

Texas is the top oil-producing state in the nation.

POPULATION

About 55 percent of Texans are white. People from Germany and France came to live in Texas in the 1800s. The Cajun and Creole people in eastern Texas have French ancestors.

Spanish people brought their language and customs to the area. About 28 percent of the people in Texas are of Hispanic heritage. Many people who live near the Texas and Mexico border speak both Spanish and English.

Population by Ethnicity

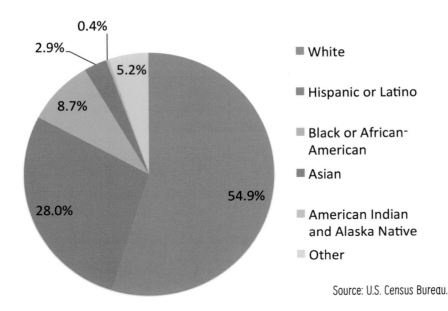

- White
- Hispanic or Latino
- Black or African-American
- Asian
- American Indian and Alaska Native
- Other

0.4%
2.9%
5.2%
8.7%
54.9%
28.0%

Source: U.S. Census Bureau.

African-Americans make up more than 8 percent of the Texas population. Many of their families came to Texas as slaves before the Civil War.

The state has three American Indian reservations. But the American Indian population in Texas is less than 1 percent.

Less than 3 percent of Texans are Asian. Men came from China to help build railroads in the late 1800s.

FAMOUS PEOPLE

Rick Riordan (1964–) is best known for writing the series of books called *Percy Jackson and the Olympians*. He grew up in San Antonio.

Sam Houston (1793–1863) led Texans to victory in the Battle of San Jacinto (1836), which gained Texas' independence from Mexico. Houston was the first president of the Republic of Texas. Later he was governor of the state of Texas.

Stephen Austin (1793–1836) started the first colony of U.S. settlers in Texas. He led the movement for Texas independence. He is called the Father of Texas. He was born in Virginia.

Sandra Day O'Connor (1930–) was the first female judge on the U.S. Supreme Court. She was born in El Paso. She joined the Court in 1981.

Nolan Ryan (1947–) was a champion baseball pitcher. He played for both the Houston Astros and the Texas Rangers. He was famous for his fastballs. He set the all-time record for no-hitters and for strikeouts. He was born in Refugio.

George Walker Bush (1946–) was the 43rd president of the United States. He took office in 2001 and served two terms. He grew up in Midland. He was Texas' governor from 1995 to 2000.

STATE SYMBOLS

Tree

pecan

Flower

bluebonnet

Bird

mockingbird

Pepper

jalapeno

PebbleGo Next Bonus! To make a dessert using an ingredient from Texas' state tree, go to www.pebblegonext.com and search keywords:

TX RECIPE

Small Mammal

armadillo

Reptile

horned lizard

Large Mammal

longhorn

Plant

prickly pear cactus

Sport

rodeo

Dish

chili

FAST FACTS

STATEHOOD
1845

CAPITAL ☆
Austin

LARGEST CITY •
Houston

SIZE
261,232 square miles (676,588 square kilometers)
land area (2010 U.S. Census Bureau)

POPULATION
26,448,193 (2013 U.S. Census estimate)

STATE NICKNAME
Lone Star State

STATE MOTTO
"Friendship"

PebbleGo Next Bonus!
To learn the lyrics to
the state song, go to
www.pebblegonext.com
and search keywords:

TX SONG

STATE SEAL

Texas adopted a state seal in 1839. One star is in the center. This star stands for the time when Texas was its own country. An oak branch and acorns are on one side of the star. This part stands for strength. An olive branch, standing for peace, is on the other side.

PebbleGo Next Bonus! To print and color your own flag, go to www.pebblegonext.com and search keywords:

TX FLAG

STATE FLAG

The Lone Star Flag was adopted in 1839. It has a white stripe above a red stripe. The white stripe stands for purity, and the red stripe stands for bravery. A blue stripe on the side of the flag means loyalty. A star is in the center of the blue stripe. It stands for Texas' independence.

MINING PRODUCTS

petroleum, natural gas, coal, Portland cement, limestone

MANUFACTURED GOODS

petroleum and coal products, chemicals, computer and electronics, machinery, food and beverage products

FARM PRODUCTS

cattle, cotton, hay, rice

PROFESSIONAL SPORTS TEAMS

Houston Astros (MLB)
Texas Rangers (MLB)
FC Dallas (MLS)
Houston Dynamo (MLS)
Dallas Mavericks (NBA)
Houston Rockets (NBA)
San Antonio Spurs (NBA)
San Antonio Stars (WNBA)
Dallas Cowboys (NFL)
Houston Texans (NFL)
Dallas Stars (NHL)

TEXAS TIMELINE

1519
Caddo, Apache, and Comanche Indians are living in the area of present-day Texas; Alonso Alvarez de Pineda of Spain sails into the Rio Grande and explores the Texas coast.

1620
The Pilgrims establish a colony in the New World in present-day Massachusetts.

1682
Spanish missions are built at Ysleta.

1685
French explorer René Robert Cavelier, known as Sieur de la Salle, is shipwrecked in Matagorda Bay. He starts a colony on the Gulf Coast.

1718
The Spanish build a fort at the mission of San Antonio de Valero.

1772 San Antonio is named the center of Spanish government in Texas.

1820 Stephen Austin leads 300 families to settle an area between the Brazos River and the Colorado River.

1821 Mexico, which includes Texas, becomes its own country.

1836 On March 2 Texas signs its Declaration of Independence from Mexico.

1836 On March 6 Texan fighters lose the Battle of the Alamo.

1836 Texas wins freedom from Mexico on May 14.

1845 Texas becomes the 28th state on December 29.

1848 The United States defeats Mexico in the Mexican War (1846–1848) and keeps Texas.

1861–1865 The Union and the Confederacy fight the Civil War; Texas fights on the side of the Confederacy.

1867–1887 Cowboys herd more than 6 million cattle from Texas to the Midwest to sell the beef.

1900 A hurricane strikes Galveston and kills more than 6,000 people.

1901 The discovery of oil on Spindletop Hill begins the Texas oil age.

1914–1918 World War I is fought; the United States enters the war in 1917.

1939–1945 World War II is fought; the United States enters the war in 1941.

1962 NASA builds the Lyndon B. Johnson Space Center near Houston to train astronauts for space flights.

1963 Texan Lyndon B. Johnson becomes the 36th president after President John F. Kennedy is killed in Dallas.

2001 Former Texas governor George W. Bush is sworn in as the 43rd president.

2005 Hurricane Rita forces more than 1 million people to evacuate Houston.

2013 The George W. Bush Presidential Center opens in Dallas in May. The center includes the former president's presidential library and museum.

2015 Texas commits to the first ever grid-connected solar power system. The grid serves 24 million Texans and provides about 90 percent of the electricity for the entire state.

Glossary

ancestor *(AN-ses-tuhr)*—a member of a person's family who lived a long time ago

census (SEN-Suhss)—an official count of all the people living in a country or district

communicate *(kuh-MYOO-nuh-kate)*—to share information, thoughts, or feelings

evacuate *(i-VA-kyuh-wayt)*—to leave an area during a time of danger

executive *(ig-ZE-kyuh-tiv)*—the branch of government that makes sure laws are followed

fertilizer *(FUHR-tuh-ly-zuhr)*—a substance added to soil to make crops grow better

heritage *(HER-uh-tij)*—the culture and traditions of one's family, ancestors, or country

industry *(IN-duh-stree)*—a business which produces a product or provides a service

legislature *(LEJ-iss-lay-chur)*—a group of elected officials who have the power to make or change laws for a country or state

loyal *(LOY-uhl-tee)*—the quality of being true to something or someone

petroleum *(puh-TROH-lee-uhm)*—an oily liquid found below the earth's surface used to make gasoline, heating oil, and many other products

Read More

Ganeri, Anita. *United States of America: A Benjamin Blog and His Inquisitive Dog Guide.* Country Guides. Chicago: Heinemann Raintree, 2015.

Kleinmartin, Hex. *Texas: The Lone Star State.* It's My State! New York: Cavendish Square Publishing, 2015.

Lanser, Amanda. *What's Great About Texas?* Our Great States. Minneapolis: Lerner Publications, 2015.

Internet Sites

FactHound offers a safe, fun way to find Internet sites related to this book. All of the sites on FactHound have been researched by our staff.

Here's all you do:

Visit *www.facthound.com*

Type in this code: 9781515704317

 Check out projects, games and lots more at
www.capstonekids.com

Critical Thinking Using the Common Core

1. What are the three largest cities in Texas? (Key Ideas and Details)

2. Hurricane Rita forced more than 1 million people to evacuate Houston. What does evacuate mean? Hint: Use your glossary for help. (Craft and Structure)

3. Texas has the most cattle of any state. How much of the state's farmland is used for cattle ranches? (Key Ideas and Details)

Index